—THE ANSWER IS—

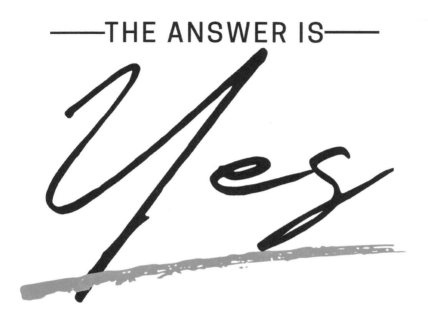

A STORY OF HOPE AND COURAGE FOR EVERYONE AND ANYONE WHO DESIRES TO DO SOMETHING MEANINGFUL FOR GOD

The Ministry Story of God's Pit Crew

Randy and Terri Johnson
with James E. Cossey

ISBN 978-1-0980-3407-8 (paperback)
ISBN 978-1-0980-3408-5 (digital)

Christian Faith Publishing, Inc.
832 Park Avenue
Meadville, PA 16335
www.christianfaithpublishing.com

Printed in the United States of America

Contents

Lord, my prayer is that the contents of this book become more than just words on a page, more than stories in a chapter.

May the contents of this book be life-changing, encouraging, challenging. Let those who read it understand that You have a plan and purpose for their lives, and may they use that plan and purpose to do something great for You.

—*Randy and Terri Johnson*

Dedication

Randy and I stand amazed that twenty years ago, God chose to use two simple people like us who set out with our children and two other families to deliver supplies to the storm victims in Oklahoma. Little did we know that this journey would be a setup for a greater plan bigger than either of us could have ever imagined.

From the simple words Randy prayed that Sunday night, "Lord, if you can use me, use me," to the God's Pit Crew that we see and love today, we stand together in agreement that we give God all the glory and honor for allowing us to be a part of his great plan to help his people by leading this amazing Christian organization.

God's Pit Crew would not be where it is today if it had not been for the hundreds of dedicated and faithful volunteers and staff who believed in our mission that with God's help and direction, we can bring hope, healing, and restoration to hurting people in times of crisis. Words could not express how thankful Randy and I are for the countless hours served and the millions of selfless acts of kindness we have had the privilege to watch unfold.

Randy and I will be forever thankful for the leadership, guidance, and wisdom of Pastor Tim and Sharon Nuckles, as well as the numerous mentors that God has strategically placed in our lives to help guide us with the growth and development of this ever-changing ministry. It has been said that some people come into our lives for a season, some for a reason, and some for a lifetime. I do believe a lifetime would be true for this couple who have stood by our side since the birth of God's Pit Crew.

To our children, we would like to say that we love you and thank you for putting up with our crazy schedule and the demands that come along with ministry. We want each of you to know how proud we are of you, and that we believe in and support you just as our own parents have been instrumental in the molding of our lives because of their strong belief in us. Our prayers for you are that you will follow God with all your heart and walk out your calling and live a life full of love, grace, and lots of laughter.

Foreword

The word *yes* is a powerful word, especially when it is spoken to us from the Lord or when spoken from us to him in response to his call.

In 1999, Randy Johnson knelt at an altar and asked God, "Can you use a person like me?" Randy was concerned about certain preconceived conditions that he might not quite measure up to, at least not in his own mind. His concern was deep. And real. He sincerely wondered, "God, can you use me?"

God's answer was *yes!*

Two weeks later, much to Randy's surprise, God called on him to respond to an almost unfathomable need after an F5 tornado ripped through Moore, Oklahoma. Randy's answer was *yes!*

The Answer Is Yes is the story of how God called and raised up a most unlikely couple to do great things for his kingdom. It is more than the story of an average couple who said yes to the prompting of the Holy Spirit; it is a story of hope and courage for anyone and everyone who desires to do something meaningful for God.

I have personally known Randy and Terri for many years, and it has been my joy to watch this amazing journey unfold. I have seen firsthand how God can take the willing hands and hearts of ordinary people and mold them into heroes for the kingdom of God.

As you read the pages of this story, you will discover again and again that the ministry of God's Pit Crew is nothing less than miraculous! It is, in fact, the story of one miracle after another.

And it all began when someone said *yes!*

Timothy Nuckles
Lead Pastor
Mercy Crossing Church

Acknowledgment

Dr. James E. Cossey, a seasoned writer and long-term ministry leader in his denomination, served as the cowriter with Randy Johnson in the development and writing of this book. A former editor in chief at Pathway Press and former editor of the Church of God's *Evangel* magazine, Cossey diligently sought in this process to adequately convey the passion of Randy and Terri for this ministry and to herald the many accomplishments made possible only by the insatiable commitment of each member of God's Pit Crew and its volunteers.

"One of the truly meaningful high points of my life and ministry has been the privilege to be involved in the development of this book. Myrlene [my wife] and I cherish our time in Danville with the Johnson's and the Pit Crew leadership. I literally wept as I reread the manuscript and saw again the tremendous level of commitment demonstrated by the people of God's Pit Crew. Our lives will never be the same," said Cossey.

Kathryn Davis is a longtime friend and volunteer of God's Pit Crew. She has traveled and served with God's Pit Crew on building projects as far away as Port-au-Prince, Haiti, as well as numerous projects in Danville, Virginia. Kathryn worked for more than a dozen years as a radio news reporter, winning multiple awards for her journalism. She also has an extensive background in writing, recording and producing radio commercials and programs, as well as knowledge and involvement in many other publications.

When Kathryn learned that it was Randy Johnson's dream to write a book, she pushed through hectic schedules and numerous other obligations to do the research and obtain the information needed to lay the solid foundation of this production. Without her heart and dedication, this book would have never been a reality. Her expertise is invaluable to God's Pit Crew, and we are grateful for the time and creativity that she poured into this project.

"Each of you should use whatever gift you have received to serve others, as faithful stewards of God's grace in its various forms."

1 Peter 4:10 (NIV)

Chapter 1

TO SERVE OR NOT TO SERVE

William Shakespeare's renowned fictional character, Hamlet, spoke those oft-quoted lines, "To be or not to be, that is the question!" Multitudes still ask that question today!

For Randy Johnson, common man and son of the Commonwealth of Virginia, this question was and is a nagging one. How does one pick up the pieces of a broken life, put it all back together again, and become what his or her God-given gifts and talents would suggest? During the past twenty years of benevolence ministry, Randy and his wife, Terri, have met innumerable individuals and couples who sincerely want to do something positive with their lives but who have wrongly concluded that because of past mistakes and accumulated bad choices, they are either extremely limited or excluded altogether. Many of these find themselves sitting out the game, sidelined linebackers, quarterbacks, star pitchers, and even potentially great coaches reduced to mere spectators. Their question is, "To be or not to be?" More directly, "To serve or not to serve?"

Such is the story of Allen, a young man that Randy Johnson often refers to in his preaching and teaching. Born and reared in a good home by a loving family, Allen began, at a young age, to make wrong choices. Both of Allen's parents were hard-working people who taught him right from wrong, instilling in him positive virtues and challenging him to properly develop and use his God-given potential. In spite of that, Allen developed issues that led to problems that plagued him all the way through high school and beyond. Allen often quipped that in his senior year, he would have been voted the "most unlikely to succeed."

Allen developed a serious aversion to work. Because he would not keep a job, he either didn't or couldn't take care of his obligations and continually bounced from one bad situation into another. Just out of high school and having begun to drink heavily, Allen moved out of his parent's house, went to work on third shift, and on most days would come home from work and drink 190-proof Everclear until he passed out.

Allen recalls an evening when his dad paid him a somewhat unwelcomed visit. Dad had come to pour out his heart about how worried he and his wife were about their son. Dad begged Allen to come back home and to get his life straightened out, but Allen refused and continued his downward spiral toward death and destruction! Soon afterward, he was introduced to illicit drugs, and the devastation grew worse.

In telling Allen's story, Randy Johnson recalls how shortly after that unsuccessful visit from his dad, Allen's mother became seriously ill and was diagnosed with cancer. Surgery was performed to remove an intestinal tumor, but the cancer spread rapidly, and she spent the better part of a full year in the hospital. Withdrawn and preoccupied in his own little world, Allen rarely came to see his dying mother. In fact, Allen recalls that the last conversation he had with his mom was in her hospital room.

Looking back, Allen can hardly believe that he did what he did and lived like he did, but he recalls visiting his mother lying in her hospital bed, weak and emaciated from cancer, and him asking her if she could help get him out of another mess that he had gotten himself into. After all, Allen's mother had always been there for him. She was his mother. He was her son.

She had always helped bail him out. It never occurred to Allen that the day might come when she would no longer be there for him. Allen's world revolved around Allen!

He never got to talk with his mother again after that day. On the few subsequent occasions that he saw her, she was unable to speak and apparently did not so much as recognize who he was. It was only a few days later that Allen's mother died a horrible, convulsive, and painful death. Allen has often been haunted by the fact that he had scores of opportunities to have visited with his mother but blew them off. Now he would never have the chance again.

He often asks himself if she died wondering if her son, whom she loved so dearly, would ever get his life straightened out.

In telling the story of Allen and others like him, Randy Johnson's desire is to show everybody how abundant God's grace is and how God not only forgives our foolish sins but transforms our lives as well. Regardless of how deep in sin one may have wandered or how many wrong paths they've taken, there is no sin that God cannot forgive, and no hurt that heaven cannot heal. For the past two decades, Randy and Terri have specialized in joining hands and hearts with broken people who feel that because they have blown it so badly, they are unfit for service. These are they who ask, "To serve or not to serve?"

But back to Allen's story!

Allen was married for the first time at age eighteen, a marriage that lasted less than a year. By the time he turned twenty-one, he had filed bankruptcy, leaving everybody he owned holding the bag and paying the price of his misdeeds. Continuing heavily into illicit drugs, he found a job driving a truck and discovered that with the aid of crystal meth, he could stay awake and literally drive for days without stopping. Meth soon advanced to cocaine, and at times, he would get so high while driving that he would literally chew on bottle lids until his mouth became one gigantic sore which he hardly felt because of the drugs.

At age twenty-two, Allen married for the second time and soon had two children although he continued to live a life filled with sin, bad choices, and foolish mistakes. Even though from time to time he would try to get his life together, he just couldn't seem to get away from the pull and pressure of the life he had chosen to live. There were times when Allen sensed that someone was watching over him. An unidentified presence. Could it be that his mother's and father's prayers were being answered even though she was now gone? Though others had given up on him and often he had given up on himself, had God not given up on him? Allen's addiction was real, and he discovered firsthand that sin takes you farther than you ever wanted to go and keeps you longer than you ever intended to stay!

Allen recalls making a run from California back to the Northeast, pushing himself to stay awake until he could unload in Massachusetts and head home. As he turned southward toward Virginia, Allen's head was pounding, eventually worsening to where he could barely see to drive. Making his way into a truck stop, he laid down in the sleeper thinking that he would feel better soon, but as he reclined, he suddenly felt a pressure like someone had parked a car on his chest. He was unable to breath and couldn't sit back up. What? Was this a heart attack? Was he dying? Reaching for his CB radio, he cried out for help!

With an ambulance on its way and his heart pounding out of his chest, Allen felt sure that he would never see his children again. This was it. This time, he had pushed the envelope too far. Here he was, hundreds of miles from home and from anybody he knew. Most likely he had caused all of this by his flagrant drug abuse, and now here he was dying alone. It was the most frightening moment of his life!

Arriving at the hospital, Allen heard the doctor pronounce with certainty that this was a heart attack. Although after the tests, it proved to be a less dangerous inflammation around his heart. Following a few days in ICU, Allen was released from the hospital, and although he tried, he could never again bring himself to use drugs. Every time he would even think about doing drugs, his heart would race, and panic would set in. He was only able to stop using when his fear of dying from drugs became greater than his desire to use them.

At this point in his life, Allen determined he would do better. In spite of all his efforts, however, after five years, his second marriage failed. He was divorced again. Alone and in a mess, although fearful of returning to drugs, he found his life now blurred in a bottle of alcohol. For months on end, he worked during the day and drank most of the night. Allen was at the end of his rope.

Remember that presence that Allen often felt with him? After months of futile drinking and total misery, that presence brought Allen to his knees in his living room in the middle of the night, where he cried out to God for forgiveness and mercy. Allen made a total commitment to Christ that night. As much as he had been sincere about doing life the wrong way, he was now serious about doing it the right way. It was all or nothing. Allen gave it his all.

Allen knew his personal weaknesses ever so well, and he knew that he could never walk this walk alone. He asked God to send someone who would help him keep his life straight once and for all. Boldly he even gave God a description of what this person should look like. He had read where the Bible said, "Ask and it shall be given to you" (Matthew 7:7). So he decided to take God at his word! Soon afterward, he was introduced to a strong-willed lady whom Allen describes as "not easily persuaded" and "no pushover!"

After a couple dates, "Lynn" made two things crystal clear to Allen. "If you hang out with me, you are going to go to church. There will be no drinking and no 'foolishness' with me."

Allen agreed to her terms and wisely began attending church with her, laying aside the drinking and any plans for "foolishness." He made another great decision by surrendering his life, not just in a panic prayer but in a total commitment of everything about himself—past, present, and future—to the lordship of Jesus Christ.

As surely as things had progressively fallen apart earlier in Allen's life, just so they now began to systematically fall into place as he grew in grace and in the knowledge of Jesus. Within two short years, free of drugs and alcohol, free of the bondage of past sin, Allen owned his own business, married that strong-willed, wonderful wife who also loved Jesus, and together they built a new home…and Lynn and Allen's children came to live with them!

Why, you might ask, did Randy Johnson choose to open this book with Allen's story? As you will often see as the book unfolds, the story of God's Pit Crew is the story of redemption. It's about people who have been rescued from one kind of devastation providing rescue for people victimized by yet another kind. Throughout this book, you will read and hear about people who lost everything only to have it restored by people who were motivated by nothing but love. You'll find people who once had lost everything because of past failures standing and serving on the front lines of this redemption story. You'll see hurt people helping hurting people.

So read on. Please. This story isn't about an organization, it's about people. Perhaps you will find someone much like yourself. You'll find people who build your faith in God and those who rebuild your faith in people. You'll find people who give you a reason to hope.

Who knows, you might even find Allen and Lynn again somewhere in the pages of this story!

One thing is for sure, you will find scores of wonderful people who, when confronted with the question, "to serve or not to serve?" responded with "the answer is yes!"

" I used to think you had to be special for God to use you, but now I know you simply need to say *yes*.**"**

Bob Goff

Chapter 2

WE ARE GOING TO DO WHAT?

An average benchwarmer! Churches are full of them. Faithful to attend every service, regularly learning about God and his Word, and supporting their church—these are the salt of the earth people that churches are made of. Randy Johnson had always considered himself one of them. Living the average life, Randy and Terri were co-owners of a small truck and trailer accessory and storage business, and Terri split her time between her job as an interior designer and the couple's four children. If the church doors were open, the Johnsons were there!

Randy's friendly smile and his successful business personality constantly provoked him to find ways to do more than just be a professional church goer, but with every prompting, he would find himself making excuses as to why just "doing the best I can" was really doing the best he could. Although he felt called to do more, perceived inadequacies held him back. "I don't know the Bible well enough," he would think, or "I don't have the skills to be a teacher or a leader in the church."

It was an otherwise normal Sunday night in 1999 when as always, the Johnson family was in church. At prayer time, Randy found himself on his knees in the altar torn between his fear of failure and a festering passion to do something that would make a difference. Crying out to God, he exclaimed, "Lord, here I am! If you can use me, please use me!" Simple enough. Straightforward. No fancy words. All on the line. If God heard his prayer, there was no notable response. No thunder crashing, no lightening, and no earthquake. Randy got up from the altar as always, and the Johnson's headed home like any other Sunday night before.

A few days later, turning on the television news, Randy learned of a horrific F5 tornado that had ripped through Moore, Oklahoma, heaping devastation and carnage all over the metropolitan areas of Oklahoma City with winds in excess of anything ever measured before. A total of 8,132 homes, 1,041 apartments, 260 businesses, 11 public buildings, and 7 churches were damaged or destroyed that day. Thirty-six people were dead. The din and drivel of the commentator's voices somehow faded into some inexplicable no man's land as Randy heard a voice saying to him, "You can help!"

"Who me? I can help?" Randy struggled with that for a day or two, pondering how a small business owner in Danville, Virginia, could possibly help tornado victims so far away. Randy was discovering that our deepest fear is often our fear of inadequacy. His reluctance suggested that whatever help he could provide would be so minimal that it wouldn't matter. If what little he could do would make little difference, why even bother? But God had other plans.

Sitting behind the store counter the following morning, gazing out the showroom window, Randy's eyes suddenly focused on a row of brand-new enclosed trailers that he had for sale. An idea invaded his thoughts! What if he used one of those trailers for ministry? After bouncing the idea around for a while, Randy responded, "Okay, God." He ultimately conceded, "I'll take that twenty-foot trailer and somehow someway, I'll fill it with supplies, and then Terri and the kids and I will take a week's vacation, and we'll take it to Oklahoma!" *Yes, Lord*, thought Randy, *the answer is yes!*

Randy could hardly wait to get home that night and share his plan with Terri, just certain that she would immediately be on board with the idea. After all, he surmised, she'd been in church all her life. This godly woman surely had a direct link to God. Excitedly unveiling his new idea to his wife, Randy was taken aback at least momentarily by her response, "We're going to do what?"

Visionaries often know where they want to go but usually need help in developing a plan to get there. In Randy's mind, the trailer was already loaded and on its way. Emotionally he was parked in Oklahoma and unloading the stuff. Both he and Terri were trying to be like Jesus!

Randy was saying, "According to your faith be it unto you" (Matthew 9:29), and Terri was thinking like Jesus did when he talked about counting the cost before building the tower (Luke 24:48). Her logical questions were, "Where on earth will we get enough stuff to fill a twenty-foot trailer?" And "how much gas will it take?" And more importantly, "Where will we get the money!" Randy's simple but faith-filled response was, "I don't know. But for once in my life, Terri, I feel like this is something God is calling us to do, and I'd like to try!"

Terri agreed. A phone regimen began. Calling local churches and businesses, the Johnson's were overwhelmed that in a matter of a few days, they had not only filled the twenty-foot trailer but had enough to fill two additional forty-eight-foot trailers borrowed from friends. When others began to hear what the Johnson's were planning, donations began pouring in resulting in more than enough to pay for all of the expenses, including the fuel, to go to Oklahoma and back!

As the day of departure approached, two other couples, Clyde and Carolyn Mangrum and Lisa and Tommy Willis Jr., and their families volunteered to make the trip using their trucks to pull the other two trailers. Loading up in Danville, the caravan headed out on the long 1,200-mile trek to Oklahoma's devastated midsection on a mission to serve, not fully grasping what God was birthing in them on this original run.

Arriving in Oklahoma, the devastation was almost incomprehensible. It was a devastation that provokes one to tears! These were fellow human beings just like each of them; they all agreed. Delivering their supplies to a local church for distribution, the team felt like their contribution that had seemed like so much when putting it together amounted to so little when compared to the situation. Weeks later, they learned that more than five hundred families had been helped.

From a simple, unpretentious Sunday night prayer in Danville, Virginia, to a devastated community in Moore, Oklahoma, Randy discovered what God can do with a simple prayer, "Lord, here I am. If you can use me, please use me!"

Surveying the devastation in Oklahoma, Randy was absolutely sure that he had made the right choice when he said, "The answer is yes!"

" The prayer of a righteous person is powerful and effective."

James 5:16 (NIV)

Chapter 3

"YES" CAN FIX THIS

"What are you going to do about it, Randy?" A stinging question was posed to Randy Johnson by one of his customers upon hearing about the double whammy impact of Hurricanes Dennis and Floyd on the Carolina coast. Adding insult to injury, the man continued, "You went halfway across the country to help those people in Oklahoma, and these are our neighbors, just a couple hours away. Why would you not help them?"

Randy had considered his trip to Oklahoma as a one-time deal, like a once-in-a-lifetime opportunity. He had responded to God's call, loaded up the supplies, and dutifully delivered them to the designated place. His work was done. Back home in Danville, life was now back to normal until this customer's deafening question!

Just as with the Oklahoma tornadoes, Randy had watched the television coverage of the Carolina storms with that same mixed sense of awe and helplessness. Early on August 30, Hurricane Dennis had peaked with winds of 103 miles per hour as it skirted the coastline. The next day, the storm interacted with a cold front and erratically moved offshore. On September 1, the storm began to collapse, but the respite was short lived as the warm Atlantic waters produced a resurgence causing it to once again turn northward and blast Cape Lookout, North Carolina, on September 4 as a strong tropical storm claiming six lives and inflicting millions of dollars in damages in its path.

Before cleanup could commence following the September 9 dissipation of Dennis, yet another tropical menace named Floyd was targeting the eastern United States. Hurricane Floyd, which had formed on September 7 off the coast of Africa, was the sixth named storm and the fourth hurricane of the 1999 season. Although initially predicted to pummel its way across Florida, it struck the Bahamas instead and, with peak strength, ransacked the island nation. Having made landfall in the Bahamas, Floyd turned northward, traveling as if guided on a predetermined path, directly up the eastern seaboard, causing massive evacuations from Florida to the mid-Atlantic states. Although weakened by its Bahamian detour, Floyd made landfall again on September 17 in the region of Cape Fear, North Carolina, dumping torrential rainfall on lowlands already saturated by Dennis, recording fifty-one Carolina fatalities and billions of dollars in damage.

As Randy pondered his customer's question, his mind raced over the news stories that he had just seen, and suddenly those same emotions that had pushed him and his team westward to Oklahoma a few months earlier were rising up within him. Randy knew what he must do! A few phone calls later, he and a few friends were loading up one of his trucks with the needed supplies and heading toward Greenville, North Carolina, to connect with Pastor Kevin McDaniel, a Danville native and pastor of the Greenville's Grindle Creek Church of God.

Randy's truck was unloaded, and the Danville crew were about to head back to Danville. Once again, as in Oklahoma, their work was done. Mission accomplished. Time to go home. Pastor Kevin, however, suggested that before they left, perhaps they'd like to have a tour of the devastation and even meet some of the families affected by it.

Reminiscent of Oklahoma, Randy couldn't believe what he saw! The horrors of devastated people and property were overwhelming! Everywhere he looked, he saw once lovely houses that had been submerged under six to seven feet of floodwaters now overlaid with messy mud and mold, emitting an unbelievable and unforgettable stench.

Billions of dollars in property damage had been sustained in North Carolina, but the greatest damage was not inflicted on brick and mortar or paint and plaster but on human lives. Thousands were displaced, and behind the ruined, rancid, and devastated houses, there were as many stories of human suffering and sorrow. As Pastor Kevin drove the Danville team around the neighborhood, hardly did they realize that the sympathy they had been feeling so far was about to morph into an empathy unlike anything that any of them had ever experienced before.

Pastor Kevin drove the team up to one particular house where they parked on the street because the driveway was heaped with what appeared to be trash and debris. Exiting the car and walking toward the house, they observed that the pile in the driveway consisted of muddy and ruined clothes, shoes, pictures, furniture, cabinets, and carpet. Just beyond the debris pile and under the carport, an elderly white-haired gentleman was sitting in a metal folding chair, his work-worn hands propped on his cane.

"This is Brother Paul Bess," said Pastor Kevin. "He's eighty-two years old, his wife died less than a year ago, and now he has lost everything to this storm." The pastor explained that the old gentleman had no children and very little family in the area.

Aware that there was no electricity or water in the house, Randy's question seemed quite logical at the time. "Why is he here?" he asked with concern. Pastor Kevin responded that this is the old man's home, the only home he knows or has. Mr. Bess had built the house himself with his own hands, and it had sheltered him and his late wife over the years. It was here that together they had lived and loved and laughed and cried and prayed together. The pastor went on to explain that since the tragedy, Brother Bess had been sleeping each night at the home of one of the Grindle Church members but gets up early each morning to make his way back home, where he sits from daylight until dark.

Inside the tiny six-room house, Randy observed that nothing of that once happy house remained except concrete floors and two-by-four walls saturated with mud and mold. The pile in the driveway outside? Well, that was a pile that consisted of all the tangible things this man had worked all his life to accumulate. Randy's heart ached as he surveyed the situation. Overwhelmed, he asked Pastor Kevin to drive him and his team back to the church. It was growing late. They needed to head back to Danville. They needed to be home by suppertime.

Randy was about to once again pass by that muddy pile in Mr. Bess's driveway when he heard the door squeak open behind him. He turned to meet eyes with Mr. Bess.

"Son," said the kind old gentleman, "would you come back inside and pray with me before you go?"

Back inside the house, the group formed a circle and closed their eyes. Before anyone else could utter a sound, Brother Bess began to pray. He talked to God in that room as if he were talking to his close personal friend—as if they had talked like this many, many times before. Standing inside his dilapidated house, this man who had seemingly lost everything thanked God for his faithfulness and praised him as a wonderful, powerful, almighty God.

Randy loved the Lord. He knew God is faithful. He knew all the right things to say at a moment like this, but in spite of it all, he found himself thinking, "Man, are you crazy?" He wanted to remind the old brother that everything he'd ever worked for was heaped in a pile on his driveway. He wanted to say, "Man, your wife is dead. Your house is destroyed, and though I mean you no disrespect, I don't see much that you've got to praise God for!" But he didn't, and the gentle old man continued his heartfelt prayer. As Brother Bess continued his prayer and as Randy listened, the Holy Spirit spoke quietly into his heart just as he had done with Oklahoma and said, "Randy, we can fix this for Brother Bess."

A man's man as he considered himself to be, Randy held back his tears as they headed home, not wanting to appear to be a wimp to his friends. As he arrived at home, however, and sat down for dinner with his family, he could hold it back no longer. Strong pent-up emotions together with the anointing of the Holy Spirit welled up inside him, finding release through a flood of tears that he unashamedly allowed to flow in the presence of his wife and children.

As the kids and his wife inquired as to what this all meant, Randy responded that he feels so guilty sitting at a table with plenty of food to eat with beautiful pictures on the walls and comfortable beds to sleep in.

"But," he explained, "we have each other. While just a few hours down the road, there's this man…"

What Randy thought he had heard while standing there in Brother Bess's house proved to truly be the voice of God. Before that first night back home had ended and Randy had pillowed his head to try and get some badly needed rest, he knew that it was indeed the Lord who had said, "Randy, we can fix this for Brother Bess."

Over the next eight weekends, Randy and a group of volunteers drove back and forth to Greenville and rebuilt Brother Bess's home. As they worked long, hard hours, the old man was right there with them, leaning on his cane and repeatedly assuring them what a wonderful blessing they were to him. As the men worked, Brother Bess talked about God's faithfulness and quoted scripture. During these working conversations, Randy learned that Brother Bess had told his friends that what he wanted more than anything else was to spend one more Christmas in his home. When God said, "Randy, we can fix this for Brother Bess," he meant to make that wonderful old man's dream come true. Brother Bess, along with all the furnishings needed to make it a home again, moved back into his fully renovated home just before Christmas.

"Let's don't make this our last mission," said one of the volunteers as they headed back to Danville following the final touches on Brother Bess's home.

"Yes," said another, "why don't we just keep doing this?"

They talked it over on the road that day, agreeing that they each wanted to keep responding to disasters, and that they wanted to continue to help put broken lives back together.

"Can we keep doing this?" they asked each other.

"Should we?"

Unanimously, they all agreed, "The answer is yes!"

Thus, God's Pit Crew was born.

"The moment when you want to quit is the moment when you need to keep pushing."

Unknown

Chapter 4

A DRIPPING POPSICLE

Randy Johnson could hardly believe he spoke these words, and of all persons, he was saying them to God.

"I'm sorry, Lord, but I quit. It's just too much of a struggle," he told the Lord as he wrestled with the passion in his soul for God's Pit Crew while trying to find a way to do the ministry and support his family. Little did he realize it at the moment, but Randy and Terri were walking through 1 Peter 1:17, "These trials will show that your faith is genuine. It is being tested as fire tests and purifies gold—though your faith is far more precious than mere gold. So when your faith remains strong through many trials, it will bring you much praise and glory and honor on the day when Jesus Christ is revealed to the whole world" (New Living Translation). This struggle would eventually prove itself to be a pivotal moment in his life and ministry.

When 2004 rolled around, God's Pit Crew had been delivering hope to disaster victims for nearly five years, and the ministry was growing. With its growth came new demands and new challenges. Randy was still working full time, six days a week in his business, and devoting an additional fifteen to twenty hours to the ministry. His required time away for the ministry put more work on Randy's business partner, and Randy's nature was to always carry his fair share of the load. The logical thing to do would be to leave the business and devote his time exclusively to the ministry, but then there was the house payment and the needs of his family to consider.

As tensions grew at work because of his divided allegiance, Randy struggled even more to balance the responsibilities of the business and his calling. One evening, on his drive home from work, his thoughts turned as they often did to his wife, Terri. Panoramic photographs raced through his mind of their life together, especially in recent years. He recalled her successful years as an interior designer, developing a good-paying job with wonderful people. He reminisced how Terri had spent months in prayer about an offer to leave her job and become the full-time children's pastor at their local church, a decision she had gladly made in order to fulfill God's will for her life.

God, is this what you are expecting from me? Randy pondered.

This drive-time conversation with God came at a time when Randy was as near to total exhaustion as he had ever been in his life. His defenses were down. His vision was clouded for the moment. That's when he cried out, "Lord,

I'm exhausted! I've got to do one or the other—either this business or the ministry. Since my job pays the bills and puts food on my table, I have no choice. I'm sorry, Lord, but I quit!"

Arriving home, Randy was met at the door by four-year-old Jarrett, the couple's youngest son. Randy recalls that Jarrett was eating a cherry Popsicle that was slowly melting and beginning to drip as he slurped it joyfully. Quickly hugging his daddy's leg, Jarrett turned and trotted into the kitchen. Randy followed and sat down on a kitchen stool. As Terri took Randy's dinner out of the stove and placed it on the counter in front of him, little Jarrett hopped up on the stool next to his dad. Randy began to nervously stir his food, wondering how he would tell Terri his decision to give up the ministry of God's Pit Crew. After all he had put his family through over the first five years of this ministry, Randy knew in his heart that Terri, his godly praying wife who always prayed through every situation, would not respond well to his idea of giving up.

Before Randy could say a word, Terri broke the silence.

"Randy," she said while choking back her tears, "I never should have quit my job and taken this position at the church. I have made a big mistake!"

Shocked, Randy retorted, "But, Terri, you are doing a fabulous job! Those kids love you."

"No, I'm not. Those kids deserve so much better than me. I don't have enough education or experience," said Terri as Randy listened in stunned silence.

"But you prayed it through, Terri. You are doing a phenomenal job. I believe it's what God has called you to do," Randy finally responded. For at least fifteen minutes, Randy diligently and compassionately sought to console his wife, trying his best to convince her not to quit, all the while feeling like something inside of his own soul was dying because he was trying to quit also. Little Jarrett just sat there quietly licking his Popsicle.

Just then Randy had an idea! *Terri has just given me a way out*, he thought. *I'll just tell her that I'm quitting too, and then we can just throw in the towel together!* As Randy pursed his lips to turn his thoughts into words, little Jarrett looked up from his Popsicle for a moment and then gazed down at the tiny bit of red liquid that was left of his cherry-flavored treat and exclaimed, "Look, Daddy! That looks like the blood of Jesus! He died on the cross, and he bled and died for me, didn't he, Daddy?"

Jesus once said, "Out of the mouth of babes God has ordained strength" (Matthew 21:16).

In that moment, Randy and Terri both instantly understood. No matter how hard they had to work or what sacrifices had to be made, nothing that either of them ever could do would ever compare to what the Savior had done for them. They vowed to God and to each other that night that they would never give up God's Pit Crew, and Terri would continue in children's ministry. Together they would each be faithful to the ministry to which God has called them.

William Cowper is credited with the words *God moves in mysterious ways his wonders to perform*, and Randy and Terri saw that as they continued for several months to wrestle with that final step of faith that would take Randy full time to God's Pit Crew. In 2005, Randy became very ill and required surgery.

Most of Randy's recuperative hospital hours were spent contemplating his future and bargaining with God.

"Lord," Randy said softly, "no matter what it takes, if you'll get me through this, I'll do what you have called me to do."

God did bring him through, and Randy kept his promise. On August 1, 2005, Randy walked away from the business he had spent years helping to build, and with no guarantee of a salary, the Johnsons trusted God to take care of all of their needs! For more than twenty years, every bill has been paid, and not one house payment has been missed.

Where might the Johnson family and God's Pit Crew have been were it not for the sweet innocence of a four-year-old and a dripping cherry Popsicle?

" Being confident of this, that he who began a good work in you will carry it on to completion until the day of Christ Jesus."

Philippians 1:6 (NIV)

Chapter 5

KMART AND KATRINA

When Randy and Terri Johnson decided to sell their business and go full time with God's Pit Crew, some of their best friends cautioned them that they might be making a big financial mistake.

"You sir, have just made the most foolish decision of your life," said their longtime personal friend and legal advisor. The Johnsons found themselves literally walking through 1 Corinthians 1:27, "But God has chosen the foolish things of the world to confound the wise; and God has chosen the weak things of the world to confound the things which are mighty." Indeed, selling—practically giving away—a business, they spent more than a decade building made absolutely no sense to most people.

The days following the closing of the sale of the business turned into a series of life-changing whirlwinds literally and figuratively! The ink had hardly dried on the contract when Hurricane Katrina struck the United States Gulf Coast in all her devastating fury! Almost two hundred-square miles were affected by Katrina, inflicting tragedy either directly or indirectly on no less than fifteen million people. When the storm made landfall near Grand Isle, Louisiana, on August 29, 2005, she was a category 3 storm with sustained winds over 127 miles per hour. Twenty-five thousand evacuees were housed at the New Orleans Super Dome, and 1,833 people lost their lives with some percent of them drowning in raging flood waters. More than one million people in the Gulf region were displaced by the storm. At their peak, hurricane relief shelters housed 273,000 people. Later, approximately 114,000 households were housed in FEMA trailers. God's Pit Crew also responded!

As the ministry was transitioning to full-time status, Randy had maintained the twenty-foot trailer they had from the beginning and had managed to secure a tractor-trailer rig and a pickup truck. These would provide the starting point for God's Pit Crew to respond to Katrina. Situated on the highly visible and easily accessible Kmart parking lot on Riverside Drive in Danville, Randy gathered volunteers and put out the word that supplies were needed. Optimistic as they were that God would supply the need, Randy and Terri could not believe what they saw! Within a day and a half, every inch of space was filled in every available means of transport, and vehicles were still backed up all the way to Riverside Drive, ready to donate water, snacks, or cleaning supplies. It was nothing short of a miracle!

One of the biggest whirlwinds of that day was the one that Randy Johnson was trying to navigate in that Kmart parking lot. Nothing he had done had prepared him for this! People were coming off every mountain and out of every holler, wanting to help. The phone never stopped ringing. People were lined up. Trucks and trailers were being filled.

Into Randy's whirlwind walked the Danville's emergency services director, Doug Young. An experienced leader, trained in emergency management, Doug knew just what needed to be done.

Taking Randy by the arm, Doug insisted, "Randy, you are coming with me!"

"But I can't go anywhere, Doug. Can't you see I'm covered up here!" said Randy.

"But you are going with me," insisted Doug Young.

Speechless and a bit confused yet compliant, Randy sat down in the car. Doug started the car with hardly another word and drove to a nearby motel where he walked Randy into an already prepared room with large white erasable marker boards and several telephones.

"Randy," said Doug, breaking the thick silence, "I want you to sit down right here. From now on, all you're going to do is make the decisions. The volunteers out there will do the rest!"

And so for hours on end, Randy directed the operation from that command post as families, businesses, churches, and corporations brought to them far more products than they could load onto the available transports. For the Johnsons, it was a mind-boggling fulfillment of Ephesians 3:20 as God provided for them "exceedingly abundantly above all that [they were able] to ask or think."

It has been said that success is a collection of problems solved, and thus, the success that took place on the Kmart parking lot that day brought with it a new set of problems to be solved. The biggest, most staggering dilemma was that with all the transport space filled, God's Pit Crew had no storage facility sufficient to house all the donated products until they could be taken to the point of need. As far back as 2002, the ministry had acquired a small space in an old abandoned tobacco warehouse, but it was far too inadequate to accommodate this! The Johnsons felt like the disciples just before Jesus fed the multitude with the loaves and fishes: "What is this among so many" (John 6:9).

As the scene on the Kmart parking lot continued to play out, the people of Danville took notice. Well-wishers showed up. Donations started coming in. People started offering advice too—often unsolicited. Some bad, some good. One such piece of good advice came from a local businessman who stuck his head in and suggested, "I believe you need some warehouse space."

Randy responded, "I believe you are right," and the man walked away only to return in a half-hour or so with an astonishing thought.

Upon his return, the businessman reminded Randy of a very large vacant facility on North Main Street in Danville, the former home of the HealthTex clothing factory, "Can you be there in fifteen minutes?"

Randy's immediate reply was "Yes, I will be there."

A few minutes later, Randy was inside the massive two hundred thousand-square-foot building, standing inside the cavernous seventy thousand-square-foot first floor, staring in awe, and talking with Gerald Gibson, the man overseeing the empty property.

"I understand you need some warehouse space," Gerald posited. "Will this do?"

"Will this do?" Randy retorted, practically speechless. "Brother, this is awesome, but we couldn't even pay the light bill on this building!"

"Well, sir," said Gerald, "it is yours to use until further notice. I cannot tell you when 'further notice' will be, but until it comes, you can use the building."

Awesome was the right word! Once again, God showed up at just the right time.

Further notice did eventually come, and when it did, God miraculously provided the means whereby God's Pit Crew was able to secure the facility as its own. Today, the entire building is owned by the ministry and houses its offices, product processing facilities, and distribution center.

The "most foolish decision" of Randy Johnson's life, leaving his business and going full-time with God's Pit Crew led him to a Kmart parking lot, which took him to a command post in a local motel, then to an empty children's clothing factory that became home to the ever-expanding ministry. And by the way, the legal advisor who once suggested Randy's ministerial naivete has since apologized in light of the ministry's success. Even many of the skeptics have come to recognize that this ministry really is God's Pit Crew.

"Some people complain they don't feel God's presence in their lives. The truth is, God manifests Himself to us every day; we just fail to recognize him."

Unknown

Chapter 6

THE PRESENCE OF GOD

Someone once wrote about the biblical character Abraham saying that he was called to leave the familiar and go to a place to which he had never been, not knowing where it was, how he would get there, or what he could expect along the journey (Hebrews 11:8–9). That perfectly describes where Randy and Terri Johnson found themselves about the time Katrina dealt her devastating blows to the Gulf Coast. Originally thinking that a quick run to Oklahoma and back and a few other small projects would be the extent of their relief ministry, they now found themselves leading a massive convoy toward Mississippi without a clue about what was truly unfolding, either upon their arrival at the Gulf or in the ministry.

From the beginning, God's Pit Crew was a walk of faith. Funds were raised, products were secured, volunteers enlisted, and deliveries were made with little or no assurance of what might lie over the next mountain or around the next crook in the road. On each mission, Randy had sought out a church and pastor in the affected area and worked directly through them for setup and distribution. Such was the case with Katrina, and so the Crew pointed itself and its cargo toward Gulfport hauling relief supplies and equipment for removing debris, armed only with a couple of names and an address. No, they were not at all unlike Abraham, or for that matter, a wagon train headed into the unknown territories of frontier America. And like those before them, theirs was a mission built on faith for the journey and hope for the future.

The trip from Danville to Gulfport is almost eight hundred miles, and loaded trucks consume a lot of fuel on such a venture. Meanwhile, as the crew was headed toward the Gulf, thousands of evacuees had been headed away from there, and so the closer they got to Gulfport, the lesser available fuel became—gas stations along the route had been depleted by the outbound demands. Venturing by faith off the beaten path and by the divine assistance of the One who was guiding them on this excursion, they managed to find enough smaller gas stations to secure sufficient fuel to reach their destination. Didn't I say that this was a journey of faith?

Imagine the strange sights of Abraham or some other frontiersman as they forge through uncharted territory. As the Crew drew nearer to the Gulf, a strange phenomenon gradually unfolded before them. Little by little, they realized that the peaceful velvet night skies had grown progressively darker, and a dreadful eeriness seemed to envelop the entire freeway. No longer were there any lighted houses and businesses and no billboards or highway signage. Inching their way into the city of Gulfport, what they experienced was like something out of a spine-chilling horror movie; there were no lights, no street signs, and no normal activities. The horrible stench of death and devastation nauseatingly filled the night air. The gut-wrenching sound of helicopters wafted through the murky black night like one would expect to be heard in some far away war zone, not here in Middle America.

Arriving late at night and unable to communicate with those anticipating their coming, the Crew located the host church, parked their rigs, and slept that first night either in their trucks or on the humid South Mississippi ground.

The next morning, the Crew was greeted by the host pastor, brokenhearted at the toll this horrific storm had taken on his community and his parish. Only a person who has lived in or visited Gulfport in better times could appreciate the historic beauty of this normally pristine waterfront city—the second largest in the state of Mississippi. From massive waterfront mansions to the homes of the middle class to the shanties of the poor, devastation played no favorites. Debris had been bulldozed off the streets into piles reaching up to eight-feet high, and entire houses had been washed off their foundations, coming to rest in the middle of the street. Some houses actually had caskets in the front yard.

Although many had evacuated, some people had come back to survey their losses or to check on loved ones, and so the Crew had plenty of help to assist them.

The only available command post was the church gymnasium, so the Crew backed their vehicles through the double doors of the building as much as possible, and the workers lined up to remove the products. There were no loading docks of course, so the volunteers and the Crew formed conveyor lines much like an old-fashioned bucket brigade fighting a frontier fire. Passing the supplies from one hand to the other, one item at a time, they unloaded cleaning supplies, thousands of bottles of water, diapers, food items, and Blessing Buckets filled with toiletries, personal hygiene products, and other items that hours before were unavailable to the displaced persons of the area.

The work of God's Pit Crew didn't conclude when the last pallet of products was unloaded and setup for distribution. No, there was a loving grip around the hearts of the Crew that brought them back to Gulfport again and again in the ensuing months. For a full two years after Katrina struck, Crew members came regularly helping remove debris, cut trees, and even rebuilding two churches and four homes. Through a partnership with various trucking companies and other corporations, the Crew was instrumental in helping bring no less than fifty tractor-trailer loads of supplies to the victims of Katrina.

Standing in the painful epicenter of death and destruction during the Crew's earliest days in Gulfport,

Randy Johnson looked around and saw what he described as the "literal presence of God." Recounting the many times that he had sensed that he had felt God's presence, Randy looked on the faces of men and women, boys and girls from all walks of life, and from various faith communities. Randy watched the teamwork of people from unidentified and innumerable cities and towns who had come together as one for the common good of all. This, he sensed, must surely be what God is like. In Gulfport, Randy concluded that he had actually seen God in the faces of his fellow man. Heading home to Danville, they were reminded of what Jesus had said so long ago, "Whatever you have done to one of the least of these, you have done it unto Me" (Matthew 25:40).

"Prayer is not asking. Prayer is putting oneself in the hands of God, at His disposition, and listening to His voice in the depth of our hearts."

Mother Teresa

Chapter 7

ALL WE COULD DO WAS PRAY

It has been said that we often find the answer to our own prayers by becoming the answer to someone else's. Time and time again, Randy Johnson and the members of God's Pit Crew have found this to be true. Randy's simple prayer on that otherwise normal Sunday night in 1999 was, "Lord, here I am! If you can use me, please use me!" In the aftermath of Katrina, the Crew again witnessed answered prayer!

As mentioned earlier, the tragedies of Katrina catapulted the simple ministry of God's Pit Crew to a level previously unanticipated, and that one would have hardly considered possible. The magnitude of Katrina's devastation demanded a greater response than anything the Crew had experienced before, and all that they could muster seemed is but a drop in the bucket of the enormous need. For these reasons and more, the work of helping folks recover from Katrina required more than a trip or two. Just as Rome wasn't built in a day, neither could the Gulf Coast be restored quickly. So upon concluding the deliveries of supplies, Randy and the Crew knew they had to do more.

The storm displaced more than a million people in the Gulf Coast region. Many people returned home within days, but up to 600,000 households were still displaced a month later. At their peak, hurricane evacuee shelters housed 273,000 people, and later FEMA trailers housed at least 114,000 households. Randy and the Crew knew they had to help rebuild some homes. But how and where?

From the beginning, Randy and the Crew worked closely with local clergy and churches as their local covering. Katrina was no exception. Calling on the host pastor in Gulfport, the Crew decided to interview potential candidates for a rebuild, knowing that they could not do it all, but they had to do something! Six families, selected by the local pastor, met with Randy and the Crew for consideration. What a challenge! All six families were similarly devastated, and all six families were similarly deserving. The challenge, which prompted hard questions asked of each couple, was to determine the one family that was the least likely to be able to rebuild without outside assistance.

Robbie and Melissa Kinsey had lost their home in Long Beach, Mississippi, along with all their earthly belongings. A hardworking young couple, the Kinsey's had married and bought their first home in 2000, only to see it literally washed away by Katrina just five years later. Because the area where they had built was not in a flood zone, they had been advised that they probably didn't need flood insurance, so they had none. Since their home was destroyed by floodwaters and not by wind, they were without the funds to rebuild. Adding insult to injury, since Robbie made a living driving a delivery truck for a snack food company and since almost all of the stores to which he had made deliveries were now out of business, he had no job, and Melissa was pregnant with their first child! For Randy and the Crew, this was a no-brainer! The answer was *yes!* God's Pit Crew would rebuild the Kinsey's family home!

Along with the fresh new crop of May flowers that began to bloom amid the coastal devastation, a new crop of volunteers—fifty to sixty in all—converged on Long Beach, Mississippi, in May 2006. God's Pit Crew was there to build a house! Soon after construction began, the Crew received an onsite visit from Melissa Kinsey's parents. Having seen the devastation of their children's home, Melissa's parents were totally overwhelmed by what they were seeing now! Breaking into tears of joy, Melissa's mom related to Randy how grateful they all were for what the Crew was doing. Said she, "We were all devastated by the storm. All of us were affected. Almost all of the homes of our loved ones were impacted." She relayed that amid their mutual experiences of devastation, how totally helpless she and her husband had felt regarding Robbie and Melissa's situation. "All we could do for them was pray," she insisted with a quiver in her chin and a tear in her voice.

Instinctively, Randy responded, "Well, you did the right thing because that's why we are here!"

Then it was Randy's turn to be overwhelmed.

"All we could do for them was pray," Melissa's mother had said.

Randy pondered how magnificently the Creator of all things could work his work in response to believing prayer. How can it be? Randy had prayed a simple prayer on a 1999 Danville, Virginia, Sunday night. That prayer was once again being answered by this opportunity to be building a house in Long Beach, Mississippi, where he and the Crew were becoming the answer to the anguished prayer of a brokenhearted mother.

By the time the Crew had completed its work in Long Beach, Robbie and Melissa's new addition had arrived. Baby Emily, along with Dad and Mom, were presented a brand-new home—fully furnished and decorated with the unique touch of Terri Johnson and constructed without cost to the Kinsey's by God's Pit Crew.

A few years after the Kinsey's moved into their new home, they were visited by Randy, Terri, and the Crew. On their way to another project in Texas, the Crew had been invited to stop off in Long Beach, where they were graciously hosted by Robbie, Melissa, and Emily, now a preschooler.

Bending down to speak with Ms. Emily, Randy said, "You don't know who I am, do you?"

Her quick response was, "Sure I do! You're the man who came and rebuilt my house!"

Mother Teresa once said, "Prayer is more than asking. Prayer is putting one's self in the hands of God at his disposition." For Randy Johnson and God's Pit Crew, every single project, especially the Katrina project and the Kinsey's home, is a glowing reminder of that truth! We often find the answer to our own prayers as we say *yes* and become the answer to someone else's.

"Have I not commanded you? 'Be strong and courageous, Do not be frightened, and do not be dismayed, for God is with you wherever you go."

Joshua 1:9 NLT

Chapter 8

STICKS, STONES, AND KNUCKLEBONES

Danville, Virginia, is situated in south-central Virginia along the North Carolina border within a day's drive of two-thirds of the nation's population. When God's Pit Crew was birthed in Danville, it was obvious that this location would be a very practical base from which to develop both a regional and national outreach. Every intention was to be just that. That is until January 2010.

A magnitude 7.0 earthquake struck Haiti on the afternoon of January 12, 2010, as one more disaster in a country that had suffered from decades of political, economic, and social setbacks and inequalities. With approximately three million people affected, this earthquake was the most devastating natural disaster ever experienced in Haiti, the poorest country in the western hemisphere. Roughly 250,000 lives were lost, and 300,000 people were injured. About 1.5 million individuals were forced to live in makeshift internally displaced person's (IDP) camps. As a result, the country faced the greatest humanitarian need in its history. Randy Johnson instinctively knew that God's Pit Crew had to stretch itself beyond its previous regional and national limitations. With the Haitian disaster, the Crew went international for the first time. Partnering with other agencies like Operation Compassion and World Help, God's Pit Crew sent more than forty containers of food, clothing, and other relief supplies to the ravaged island nation.

Since its inception, God's Pit Crew has worked through local churches and relief ministries to assure that onsite distribution was fair, ethical, and equitable. In Haiti, the Crew partnered with John and Joyce Hanson and International Missions Outreach, a tried and proven ministry with a thirty-five-year track record located in Delmas, a suburb of Port-au-Prince, the nation's capital.

God's Pit Crew has never been about sending in supplies, doing a photoshoot, and leaving. It seems that in almost every disaster, God impresses upon the Crew some kind of ongoing involvement with the ministries and people of the affected area. Just as had happened with Brother Bess's little house in North Carolina, and the Kinsey's home in Mississippi, when Randy visited Delmas in May of 2010, he knew that the Crew's work there wasn't over. The following February, Randy led a crew of more than twenty-six volunteers to build eight homes and a children's playground.

Prior to the Crew's arrival for the construction to begin, Randy had arranged for the delivery of more than $50,000 worth of donated building supplies and for the pouring of the concrete slabs on which they would build houses. With this advance planning, upon arrival, Randy immediately divided the Crew into two teams, one to frame the fourteen-by-twenty-eight houses that would soon become homes to displaced elderly persons in the village of Boutin, and the other team to build a playground, a luxury previously unknown to the children of the village.

The children of Boutin, a small rural village without electricity or any amenities we consider essential like kitchens and bathrooms, had never seen a playground. The only toys with which they had ever played were homemade gadgets created by their parents, often made from scrap wood or metal retrieved from trash heaps. But Joyce Hanson or Madame Pas (short for pastor), as the Haitian people called her, longed to give them this gift that she knew they would love. Joyce had prayed fervently for twenty-five years that God would help them find a way to provide a play area for these children who had no toys except the ones they or their parents could make. Thanks to God's Pit Crew and a major donation from the people of an American company that these children would never meet; Joyce Hansen's prayers were being answered!

When the playground was completed, the children, who had never received such an extravagant gift, asked Madame Pas, "Is the playground for everyone?" Hardly could they fathom the idea that this recreational facility could be theirs.

Madam Pas responded by asking the children, "Did Jesus die for everyone or for just a few?" Of course, their answer was that Jesus died for everyone, and so Joyce explained that this beautiful playground was just like Jesus, it belonged to them all. On the day of dedication, the children played happily into the night, undeterred by the darkness, laughing and shouting joyously in the moonlight.

As the years went by, and the relationship between God's Pit Crew and International Missions Outreach (IMO) continued to grow, Terri Johnson found a way to put her love for children and her experience as a children's ministry director to work for the children of Haiti. She discovered that IMO had more than seven thousand children enrolled in its schools and/or its feeding programs. She also learned that each year at Christmas, Madame Pas had clamored tenaciously to put together enough Christmas gifts for many of these children, most of whom would otherwise receive nothing at all. Even with assistance from many churches including a Danville, Virginia church, White Oak Worship Center, Joyce simply could not come up with enough gifts.

Remember that Terri Johnson is the number one prayer warrior behind God's Pit Crew, the never-say-never interior decorator turned children's minister turned ministry partner. Terri is also the one who, way back when Randy first announced to her his interest in starting the ministry by taking supplies to Oklahoma asked, "Where will we get the money?"

Now after years of seeing God tear down walls, open doors, and provide the impossible, she dares to believe God to provide toys for seven thousand Haitian kids! Thus, the

God's Pit Crew version of the Gifts of Love program was born.

Terri's heart broke when she learned that these kids would have no Christmas gifts. She recalled how, as children, she had played the simple game of jacks, played with a tiny ball and ten metal objects or "jacks." Interestingly, the game was originally called knucklebones. It is a game of ancient origin, usually played with five small objects, or ten in the case of jacks. Originally the knucklebones (jacks) were those of a sheep, and as Terri would discover, even in the twenty-first century, these poor Haitian children played this simple game with the actual knucklebones of goats that had been slaughtered for food.

With passion in her heart and a desire to help make sure IMO had a Gift of Love present for each child, Terri's answer was *yes!* I will help the children of Haiti.

Terri began to collect a variety of items that she felt the children would enjoy, including jump ropes, baby dolls, soccer balls, toy trucks, school supplies, coloring books, crayons, as well as a bag of rice and black beans that would go in each gift. Not only would a child have a nice toy, but the family would have a meal as well. Dozens of volunteers came to the Pit Crew warehouse and sorted the items into individual bags to be sent to the Haitian children. After the program had been active for several years, a local church, hearing about Gifts of Love, gave God's Pit Crew a generous donation of $25,000, enabling Terri to buy backpacks to load up with enough gifts and toys for two thousand children and two hundred teachers and staff members at the IMO schools. That year, Terri's bags of love made it possible for Madame Pas to give Christmas gifts to every child enrolled in IMO programs and often with enough left over to give out to children on the streets.

Such has been the ongoing evolution of God's Pit Crew. From a tense dinner table meeting in 1999, when a godly but confused and concerned wife asked the natural normative question, "Where will we get the money?" to the streets of a Haitian village filled with grateful children, God has proven himself to Randy and Terri and God's Pit Crew. On that fateful night in response to his wife's passionate inquiry, Randy had said, "I don't know where we'll get the money, but for once in my life, I feel like this is something God is calling us to do, and I'd like to try." That night, Terri's answer was *yes*! She agreed with Randy and with God. She still does!

" Write down the vision and make it plain, that those who read it may understand it, and run with it."

Habakkuk 2:2

Chapter 9

BE THE BLESSING

Visitors to the Pit Crew warehouse on any given work day will find a kind, hardworking, passionate lady leading a team of volunteers gathered around what looks like a small factory assembly line. This line is covered end to end with bright-blue buckets that appear to the uninformed as nothing more than five-gallon plastic containers. Stunning yellow letters on the bucket are traced in brilliant orange with the words "This Blessing Bucket is provided by God's Pit Crew Crisis Response Team."

The sweet vivacious lady who leads this crew will take a momentary break to greet visitors who tour the facility, and she might even pray with you, but what she will not tell you is that this Blessing Bucket ministry, at the level of effectiveness that it enjoys today, was born in her heart by a divine visitation from the Holy Spirit. Her story, like every story connected to the Crew, is one of divine guidance, anointing, and favor.

Julie Post was a pediatric speech pathologist with her own practice, living the good life in southwestern Virginia. A single mom, she and her children were active in their local church. When she first heard about the ministry of God's Pit Crew, Julie was moved with compassion about what they were doing for others but really never anticipated that she would be involved in any way other than through her prayers and gifts.

Nathan Burnett, a tenured employee of the Virginia Department of Transportation, was a member of the same church, with the same burden for God's Pit Crew, although Julie and Nathan were more acquaintances than friends. That would soon change with the Crew—and the Holy Spirit largely responsible for the transition.

On April 18, 2011, three back-to-back tornadoes pummeled the city of Pulaski, Virginia, located about two hours away from Danville. The first hit came at 7:37 p.m., an EF-1 with twisting winds of up to 125 miles per hour, and a path that measured approximately 480 yards wide, extending some 2.8 miles. Miraculously no lives were lost although several were injured, and substantial property damage was realized. As could be expected, God's Pit Crew was off to Pulaski, and one of the persons recruited as a volunteer on this mission was Nathan Burnett.

Taking a short break from cleaning debris and handing out relief supplies to victims, Nathan returned to his church to share with the people about the devastation he had seen and to recruit others to go back with him to assist. Through teary eyes and from a breaking heart, Nathan emotionally shared about the scores of families whose homes had been demolished and about gigantic trees uprooted and deposited on rooftops. He passionately appealed to his fellow church members to go back with him to Pulaski and help God's Pit Crew with this gargantuan task. Julie Post and her daughter were among the first to volunteer.

Julie and Nathan talked a lot that day as they all prepared to drive to Pulaski. As time went by, they discovered that they shared many of the same interests, not the least of which was their passion for helping others. They soon came up with an idea to organize a five-kilometer run to raise money for God's Pit Crew and then together developed a communitywide drive to collect water and other relief supplies for the Crew to distribute to the victims of the next disaster—wherever that might be. Nathan and Julie began to spend more time together, then they began to date.

Ultimately, they became Mr. and Mrs. Nathan Burnett. Together they continued to designate their vacations and whatever other time they could find to God's Pit Crew.

As Nathan and Julie continued to volunteer, they soon learned about a ministry of God's Pit Crew that had been started long ago called "Blessing Buckets." Five-gallon buckets were purchased and packed with toiletries, pop-top cans of nonperishable food, hygiene products, and simple cleaning supplies. Once packed, the Crew would distribute these buckets to people affected by disasters. Nathan and Julie began to lead special drives in their church and community to collect the necessary items to fill the Blessing Buckets. Along the way, they also began to encourage the people of their local church to gather items and fill their own buckets to be delivered to God's Pit Crew.

In 2012, even though the Burnett's were actively supporting the Crew, they were not close friends with any of the leadership. Imagine Julie's reaction when one evening, she experienced a vivid and dynamic dream about the Blessing Bucket program and what seemed to almost be a mandate from God as to how the program needed to go forward. She shared the dream with only her husband whereupon they concluded that they should wait for God's timing to approach Randy or anyone from the Crew. Meanwhile, she wrote out in specific detail all of the things she had seen in her dream about the Blessing Buckets. Bathing it all in prayer, she resigned herself to the thought that if this was really a "God thing," someone from God's Pit Crew would approach her, not the other way around.

Julie said nothing to anyone else about her nighttime visitation for nearly a year. During this time, she and her church had been actively filling buckets. When they had filled a thousand buckets, Julie contacted Randy and told him that the buckets were ready. Thanking her for the hard work and making plans for their delivery to Danville, Randy ended the conversation with, "If you ever have any ideas that you'd like to share about the Blessing Buckets, I'd be glad to hear them."

In that moment, Julie's immediate answer was *yes!* Her heart skipped a beat as she replied hesitantly, "Actually, I do." Swallowing hard, she then proceeded to tell him all about her vision for the Blessing Buckets, and almost before she realized it, she uttered, "And I'd like to share it with your staff!" She was thrilled with Randy's response and his encouragement to come down as soon as possible to Danville and talk about it.

Julie was literally trembling when she came to the leadership meeting and announced to them how she felt that God wanted to do something on a much larger scale throughout multiple cities sponsored by God's Pit Crew. As Crew leaders listened intently, Julie laid out the entire dream, challenging them that "we need to fill five thousand buckets!" Gaining boldness gradually as she spoke, Julie offered the idea that they should be assembled right there in the warehouse and made available and ready for whenever the next disaster might strike.

Julie had come to the meeting not only armed with a vision, but also she had followed the same instructions given to the Prophet Habakkuk. "Write down the vision and make it plain, that those who read it may understand it, and run with it" (Habakkuk 2:2). As the Crew leaders perused the printed proposition that she had provided, John Cline, Vice President of Operations, interrupted saying, "So you are wanting us to purchase five thousand empty buckets by faith?" That was exactly what she was saying!

When it was determined that the cost would be about five dollars per bucket or a total cost of $25,000 to get five thousand buckets, John Cline looked directly at Julie and said, "You've brought us this vision and said it is from God, but what role are you willing to play in it?" Before she could parse her lips to reply, he continued, "Will you head it up?"

Over the months that had passed since Julie's dream, she had come to realize that God didn't give her the vision for her to merely pass it off to someone else. It was a vision for God's Pit Crew all right, but it had been given directly to her. The dream had been unsolicited. She didn't ask for this; God had gifted it to her! Instinctively, Julie knew that God expected her to be in the middle of it. She had no choice but to answer, "Yes, I will lead it."

Lead it she did at this first large-scale drive! Enough supplies were collected to fill all five thousand of the buckets she had proposed. Furthermore, they recruited volunteers to come to the warehouse in Danville to assemble and fill the buckets. One week later, massive floods hit South Carolina, and God's Pit Crew delivered all five thousand Blessing Buckets to the victims. Julie was in awe but not at all surprised because all of this had been revealed to her in her dream.

"Nathan," she said, "God knew that we need to be prepared. He just wanted us to be faithful to the vision."

For the next three years, Julie continued her pediatric outpatient rehabilitation practice and, although living three hours away from Danville, also led the Blessing Bucket program. During those years, the ministry continued to expand and to experience new victories, reaching new levels each year. When John Cline resigned in 2017 as Vice President of Ministry Operations, Randy offered the position to Nathan, also requesting that Julie become the first full-time director of the Blessing Bucket program. Nathan and Julie knew what they must do, but only after much prayer, the Burnett's agreed. Nathan resigned his position with the state of Virginia although he was a mere five years away from retirement with full benefits. Julie sold her practice, and the Burnett family relocated to Danville to start a new chapter in life and ministry.

The Blessing Bucket ministry is what it is today because of people who looked at the vastness of what this program could become in the future and by the tenacity of one godly couple who heard from God in a dream and who dared to help turn that dream into reality. With Julie leading the way, the Blessing Bucket program has continued to expand and, in April 2018, became international. Along the assembly line that Julie organized in the warehouse, two thousand Blessing Buckets were filled with toiletries, food items, kids' coloring supplies, and a Spanish Bible. In July 2018, the Blessing Buckets were distributed in Guatemala.

If you ever have the privilege of visiting the warehouse in Danville on a regular business day, you'll see a happy team filling Blessing Buckets and having a great time in the Lord. Everyone who comes is deeply moved by the sight. Some are moved to tears. Some can only stand and stare, hoping somehow to take it all in.

Many are amazed, not believing what they see and experience. Not Julie Burnett! Everything she is seeing now, she had already seen in the Spirit.

George Bernard Shaw once said, "You see things, and you say, 'Why?' But I dream things that never were, and I say, 'Why not?'" That quote defines the Blessing Bucket Program and Julie Burnett.

"If there's a Goliath in front of you, that means there's a David inside of you."

Carlos A. Rodriguez

Chapter 10

ONLY A BOY

Most people are familiar with King David in the Bible. We know him as the writer of the Psalms, a man who sought after God, and as Israel's king. David is first introduced to us, however, not as a king but as a young shepherd boy. The Bible tells in 1 Samuel 17 how the nation of Israel was being harassed by a terroristic, overgrown Philistine named Goliath. Every grownup who was being considered to come against the giant was either too afraid or was rejected. Then came David, who armed himself only with a sling and five stones, paraded himself in front of this mammoth-sized enemy and declared, "You are coming to fight against me with a sword, a spear and a javelin. But I'm coming against you in the name of the LORD who rules overall" (1 Samuel 17:5).

One stone brought down the giant and consequently multiple generations later, the terms, "David and Goliath," is synonymous with ordinary people overcoming what seem to be extraordinary and insurmountable circumstances.

Many who read this will recall as a child in Sunday school, Children's Church or Vacation Bible School, singing the song, "Only a Boy Named David," telling that magnificent story of David's victory. What is the bottom-line message? Simply this—never underestimate the ability of a child who dares to say *yes* and believe that the impossible is possible!

You will recall that you were introduced in chapter 3 to Randy and Terri Johnson's youngest son, Jarrett. At age four, the Holy Spirit took the simple words of an innocent child licking a cherry-red Popsicle and redirected the destiny of a family!

Unlike his older siblings who came along before the birthing of God's Pit Crew, Jarrett has grown up with the ministry. He can scarcely remember a time when God's Pit Crew was not part of him and vice versa. Walking and living by faith, packaging products, delivering Blessing Buckets, and responding to disasters are all he has ever known. Jarrett lives and loves God's Pit Crew just as his parents do!

When Jarrett was eleven years old, Randy and Terri decided to take him on a trip to Haiti. There they visited with John and Joyce Hanson and toured the many ministries of International Missions Outreach (IMO). Jarrett was exposed to a way of life that was totally foreign to him and to most children growing up in today's prosperous, affluent Western world.

The Hansons and IMO operate eighteen schools and provide basic education to impoverished Haitian children in many additional satellite schools scattered around the country, thus providing education for thousands of Haitian children. Eleven-year-old Jarrett visited several of these, and though but a child himself, he was deeply moved by the happiness and joy he observed in these students who had never experienced some of the most basic comforts that he had never had to live without.

Young Jarrett was especially touched by what he saw in one particular school, where the children were all huddled together in the center of a large, mostly dilapidated room in a building still in a state of crumble in the aftermath of Haiti's 2010 7.0 magnitude earthquake that had occurred only a few months earlier.

More than 250,000 people were killed on January 12, 2010, with 300,000 others injured and as many as five million people displaced because of the earthquake's carnage and devastation. When Jarrett Johnson saw these happy kids, learning and loving like nothing had happened, he knew that he could do something! No, he knew that he must do something.

Returning home, young Jarrett could not dismiss the scenes that were forever stored in the hard drive of his mind! In Haiti, he had seen poverty from a new perspective. Although a lad, he was exposed to scenes in the aftermath of a nation's worst natural disaster that most adults will never see. Furthermore, Jarrett was growing up in a home environment in which simply doing nothing has never been an option!

Jarrett was told that it would require $100,000 to buy land and build a new school, an amount that sounds staggeringly near impossible. However, like young David standing up against Goliath, the child was firmly convinced that there simply wasn't a problem! Was this a need or was it not? Could God make it happen or could he not? Jarrett's answer was *yes!* After all, Jarrett had grown up to this point being told repeatedly and seeing it demonstrated that "with God all things are possible" (Matthew 19:26).

Jarrett soon got his parent's permission, and it was announced that he was starting a new project called Kidz Helping Kidz. The goal of this new outreach of God's Pit Crew would be raising the money for a new school in Haiti. The Kidz Helping Kidz program was enhanced by what Jarrett called Change for Change. The word soon began to spread, and children all across the country were being encouraged to save all the coin change that they could, earmarking it for the Haitian school.

Realizing that change alone might never raise enough money to build the school, some churches began designating their Vacation Bible School and Kids Crusade offerings and sponsoring other events for the project. No doubt there were some skeptics who thought that maybe the kid had bitten off more than he could chew, but even the most negative skeptic was silenced when in less than two years, more than $25,000 had been raised.

Before the end of 2014, just three short years after Jarrett's Haiti trip, more than $60,000 had come in through Kidz Helping Kidz. This amount was enough to purchase the land and construct a twelve-foot security wall around the property. Work began and then volunteers stepped in and built an open-air shelter where the children could gather to eat their daily lunches of rice and beans and provided to them freely by International Missions Outreach.

God's Pit Crew with God's help has always been about making the impossible possible. You may recall that the first question Terri asked Randy in their first conversation about the ministry was, "Where will you get the money?" This of course is still the question with every new project with every new disaster and literally with every new day. But God provides. Every time.

Way back then, deliverance came to the people of Israel when a boy named David dared to trust God and act on that trust. In 2017, a new school was completed in Haiti because a boy named Jarrett trusted God and acted on that faith.

Jesus has a special place in his heart for children, or he would not have said, "Let the little children come to Me, and do not forbid them; for of such is the kingdom of heaven" (Matthew 19:14). Both David and young Jarrett demonstrated how God will respond to childlike faith.

Through the birth of the Kidz Helping Kidz program, young Jarrett learned valuable lessons about faith and about following through with the work ethic to make what we believe become reality. He learned valuable lessons, and today Haitian children are learning something new every day because "a little child shall lead them" (Isaiah 11:6).

"Only a Boy Named David" 1931
Arthur Arnott

Only a boy named David, only a little sling,
Only a boy named David, but he could play and sing.
Only a boy named David, only a rippling brook,
Only a boy named David, but five little stones he took.
One little stone went in the sling,
And the sling went 'round and 'round,
One little stone went in the sling,
And the sling went 'round and 'round,
And around and around and around and around
And around and around and around
One little stone went up, up, up…
And the giant came tumbling down!

"God uses imperfect people who are in imperfect situations to do His perfect will."

David Young

Chapter 11

THE REST OF THE STORY

From the very beginning, God's Pit Crew has been about the people. You will recall that it was the suffering displaced people of Oklahoma that had first pricked the heart of Randy Johnson, urging him to do something. From that fateful newscast where Randy saw the devastation sweeping across Moore, Oklahoma, to the next day, peering across the parking lot at empty cargo trailers, it was the people who were the focal point.

In this final chapter, we will focus on some of the many people who heard God's call and whose answer was *yes!* These are the people who have made it possible for God's Pit Crew to grow and to touch so many thousands of lives. As surely as Nehemiah in the Old Testament story was able to rebuild the broken-down walls of Jerusalem "because the people had a mind to work" (Nehemiah 4:6), so the establishment, growth, and expansion of God's Pit Crew has been because of men, women, youth, and children who rolled up their sleeves, went to work, and made a difference.

Remember our earlier story about Randy and Terri's son, Jarrett, and the school in Haiti? Well, interestingly enough, Jarrett isn't the only young person whom God has uniquely used through the ministry of God's Pit Crew. Fact is, God has used and is using people of all ages, races, cultures, and backgrounds.

In 2017, when nine-year-old Silas Zeidler saw pictures on the news of elderly people sitting in waist-deep water in a nursing home during Hurricane Harvey, he decided he could do something. Silas's answer was *yes!* With the help of his entire family, he made thirty-two gallons of his family's recipe of fresh-squeezed lemonade, which he served up by the glass in exchange for a donation to God's Pit Crew for their Houston response. He dubbed his project "LemonAID for Texas." By the end of the day, he had raised more than $9,000. To date, Silas's #JuicingForJesus lemonade stand had raised right at $25,000 for God's Pit Crew's various disaster relief projects. His latest endeavor was to help raise money to rebuild the Moffett School in Moffett, Oklahoma, which was flooded in May 2019. Silas and his mom, Tanya, were able to make their first disaster relief trip with God's Pit Crew in September 2019.

Silas's entire family, including his parents, grandparents, and great-grandparents, are longtime volunteers, and his uncle is an employee. His Mimi is the volunteer assistant to the vice president of advancement operations, so he has to regularly come to the office with her since the age of four. Long before he began raising money with his lemonade stand, he was stuffing envelopes, sorting coins, emptying trash, and doing odd jobs around the distribution center. Silas is now eleven-years-old and a sixth grader at the Carlisle School in Martinsville, Virginia, and says he plans to be a volunteer for the rest of his life!

Trevor Dowdy's dad is a regular volunteer, and the lad often felt left out when his dad considered him too young to accompany him on disaster relief projects. Each time Dad would leave on a trip, Trevor pleaded to go, and at age ten, he got his chance to go to a flooded area of West Virginia, where the Crew remodeled a home and did repairs to a local church. Young Trevor became addicted to the concept of helping others. He has since gone on no less than six additional projects. The passion of his young heart is to be involved in the daily operations of the ministry, but God's Pit Crew's warehouse is more than two hours away from his home.

As fourteen-year-old Ethan Newlen prepared to become an Eagle Scout, he was required to plan, develop, and execute a project that would help a local community or a nonprofit organization. A frequent listener to local Christian radio, he had often heard about the Blessing Bucket ministry of God's Pit Crew, and so he decided to raise the money and assemble one hundred Blessing Buckets.

The teenager sent out letters, e-mails, and passed out flyers, and to everyone's amazement in just over one month, Ethan had raised more than twice the needed amount for the one hundred buckets. In June 2016, Ethan's scout troop met to assemble the buckets. Two days later, Ethan and his family made the two-hour drive to Danville to deliver one hundred completed Blessing Buckets, several hundred other items they had collected, and a check for more than two thousand dollars!

David and Joanna Willis are charter members of God's Pit Crew and have each volunteered more than ten thousand hours since 1999. In the beginning of his association with the Crew, David worked a full-time job but was able to negotiate up to five or six weeks of vacation each year to the ministry. He vividly recalls one of his early trips to assist victims of Katrina. He and Joanna had gone with another couple to Gulfport, Mississippi, to survey the destruction. They were stunned by huge heaps of debris piled as high as twenty feet in the air in places where homes and businesses once stood.

Looking around Gulfport, David and Joanna observed a lonely woman slowly walking by. The lady seemed as though she was walking in a daze. When, out of his concern for her, David asked if he could help, she responded by pointing to three doorsteps sitting hauntingly alone by the side of the street.

Said she, "You see those three steps over there? That's all that's left of the house I've lived in since I was a child. I'm just looking for anything that might be left of my house."

David and others began to help her search through the rain-soaked debris, and soon David came across an eight-by-ten photograph. As he showed it to the woman, she hugged him profusely and wept so hard that her tears soaked the shoulder of his shirt.

"That," she said, "is a picture of my son. It's the only thing I have left in this world."

That moment is forever cemented in David's heart and mind. So much so that since retirement from his job, David has been a core volunteer, now serving as the warehouse manager for God's Pit Crew.

It seems that a number of people with construction backgrounds like David have been drawn to the ministry of God's Pit Crew. Another such person is Jay Setliff, a career employee at Goodyear in Danville, but one who was always involved in construction projects. His construction expertise, together with the fact that his own home was once ripped apart by a tornado, led Jay to volunteer.

When a second tornado struck Moore, Oklahoma, four years after the first one, Jay and David Willis were among the volunteers to go there and rebuild a family's home. The uniqueness of this story is that a man whose home was once destroyed by a tornado was helping rebuild the home of another family whose loss he had experienced. On the final day of the project, a television reporter asked Jay what he would say to the family of the new home.

"I hope they really live in this house and love every minute of it," said Jay.

James Hodge, another core volunteer, tells the story of a trip to a small town in Tennessee that had been devastated by a tornado in 2003. Arriving on site, James recalls a neighborhood littered with fallen trees but where most of the homes had escaped major damage.

As the Crew began cutting and clearing trees, a car was observed to slowly proceed up the street and then stop at the site where several huge oak trees had fallen. No house was visible. An elderly couple got out of the car and slowly began walking through the twisted branches. Behind and beneath those trees was a house covered over by tree limbs but virtually unscathed by the storm. The couple opened the door and went inside.

James and the other crew members began to clear away debris from near the house as a pastor, also a volunteer, went inside to converse with the couple.

Emotionally she began to speak, "I'm just now bringing my husband home from the hospital. He's been undergoing treatments for terminal cancer." She went on to explain that as they were making the drive home, they had no idea that the tornado had struck, let alone that it had done damage to their property. When asked about their relationship with the Lord, the gentleman responded that, no, he wasn't a true believer, but he said, "Preacher, I'll tell you where I see God. I see God in the men and women wearing red shirts, who would travel so far to help a total stranger like me by cutting the trees off my home."

God has called men and women like James Hodge and others whose answer was *yes* to be his church, to be his hands and feet, to be the hands and feet of Jesus, and to take his love and mercy into a dark world to minister to the lost, the poor, and the broken.

Such are the stories of the people of God's Pit Crew. From the inception of the ministry in 1999 until today, it would require volumes to tell of all the people, all the experiences, and all the special stories…stories of people who sensed that something needed to be done, and that God wanted them to do it. People whose answer was *yes!* Many of these questioned their own abilities. Thought twice. Felt unqualified. Almost didn't. But thank God they decided to serve against all odds. Before concluding this volume, however, we must come back to one other story.

In chapter 1, we introduced you to Allen, a man whom Randy Johnson refers to often in his messages. Remember Allen, who was the twice-divorced addict who, but for his late mother and father's prayers, might have thrown his entire life away through bad choices? Remember how Allen turned his life to Christ and then was led by the Holy Spirit to the one woman who could help him walk the straight and narrow a woman named Lynn?

Allen became involved in the work of God's Pit Crew from the very beginning. So did Lynn, although she was initially more hesitant to dive in than Allen was. In fact, it can be said that there isn't one single project, one single issue, or one single step on the GPC journey that has been made without either of them.

For years, Allen felt like the biblical prodigal son (Luke 15:11–32). Because of his wayward lifestyle, Allen, like the unnamed prodigal son, felt unworthy to come back home or to be so much as called a good son. But he did come home and, like so many others, realized one day that God could use him as surely as he ultimately used young Jarrett and all the others mentioned in this book.

Allen, because of his faith in God and because of a faithful pastor and a good woman whom God placed in his life, came to understand that God is like a potter who takes misshapen and broken pottery and puts it back on the potter's wheel in order to lovingly remold and reshape it (Jeremiah 18:1–12). The Holy Spirit taught Allen that when God remakes a broken vessel, it is no longer second-rate, and even though it may have some distress marks here and there because of the process, those little bumps only serve to make it a stronger vessel.

One of Allen's great concerns over the years has been that if people really knew his story, they might respect him less. That perhaps they would want to hold his past against him. He concluded though that while that fear might prove true with some, perhaps even more would respect him for his honesty and be turned toward his God, seeing what he has done in Allen's life. The one thing Allen and Lynn determined to do was to serve. They would serve God, and they would serve the less fortunate regardless of what anybody thought about them! Faced with the question, "To serve or not to serve," they both determined that serving was their only choice. Allen and Lynn determined once and for all, the answer is *yes*!

So why is Allen's story so important? Because Allen's story is the story of God's Pit Crew. In a very real sense, Allen's story is God's Pit Crew. Why is that? Because, you see, Allen's wife, the woman God sent him to lead him and keep him on the narrow path, the woman who fit every detail of Allen's prayer for a faithful life partner, that woman, sweet Ms. Lynn, is also known as Terri Lynn Johnson, and Allen is none other than Randy Allen Johnson.

"Therefore, if anyone is in Christ, the new creation has come: The old is gone, the new is here!"

2 Corinthians 5:17 (NIV)

Randy's Epilogue

When I first decided to tell Allen's story, my challenge was should I or should I not reveal Allen's true identity? I sincerely struggled with that. How would people respond to knowing that the founder and director of God's Pit Crew was that guy? The more I pondered, however, the more I knew that the answer is *yes!* I must tell it all to the glory of God!

You see, the moment I asked God for his forgiveness, he forgave every sin. He didn't just forgive some sins or just change some parts of my life, he changed everything in my life. The person I was when I went to my knees never got up again! A different man emerged! I experienced what the apostle Paul promised, "If anyone is in Christ, he is a new creation; the old has gone, the new has come" (2 Corinthians 5:16).

For any one reading this who thinks you cannot be used of God because of your past failures, bad decisions, and sins, I bring you great news! Some of the greatest people of God in the Bible were once part of a pretty rowdy bunch!

Abraham was a liar.

Moses was a murderer.

David was an adulterer and a murderer.

Peter was one who denied that he even knew Jesus.

Paul was a persecutor.

And the list goes on…By no means am I suggesting that in order to be used of God, one must go out and do bad things. Certainly not. What I am telling you is that if you have taken some wrong turns and have been down some wrong paths, that doesn't mean that you cannot turn around, and once you've turned around, it doesn't mean that God can't or won't use you.

Randy Allen Johnson made bad choices and took wrong turns. But when I came to the end of myself, I fell on my knees in my living room and found a new beginning. That new beginning was the start of a brand-new life that has kept me, sustained me, and used me until this day. Everything changed when my answer became *yes!*

You may be feeling like you are at the end of your rope and can no longer hold on. This feels like the end for you. I know how that feels. I can also tell you that your new beginning can be found at an altar of prayer when your answer to the Lord is *yes!*

The Bible says, "If you openly declare that Jesus is Lord and believe in your heart that God raised him from the dead, you will be saved. For it is by believing in your heart that you are made right with God, and it is by openly declaring your faith that you are saved" (Romans 10:9–10).

When you are ready, talk it over with God. Find a place to get alone and just talk. If you've never been a person of prayer, that's okay. Talk to him openly like a friend. I can tell you from experience, he is the best friend you'll ever know! Admit to God that you've blown it. Tell God how sorry you are for your sins. Ask his forgiveness and believe that because of what the Bible says, he will forgive you. Be specific with God about whom and what you need in your life to make a complete turnaround. Then thank him for it even though you haven't seen it all happen yet. The Bible calls this faith. Faith is about what we yet hope for and about things we have not yet seen (Hebrews 11:1).

If you need help with prayer, consider praying these words but only if you mean them,

Eternal God, I am ready to say *yes* to you! Yes, I am a sinner. Yes, I've made bad choices and foolish decisions, and I know that I can't keep going the way I'm going. I need to turn around. I need help. I openly declare that Jesus Christ is Lord, and that there is no other Lord but Jesus. I believe in my heart that God raised Jesus from the dead, and that he is my savior. You said that by this open declaration and by the faith in my heart, I can be saved. I receive that. I am sorry for my sins, and I give them up to follow you. Forgive me. Cleanse me. Change me. I receive your forgiveness, and most of all, I receive *you* into my life. I say *yes*, Lord, to your offer of eternal life. According to your Word, I am now saved. In Jesus's name. Amen.

If you prayed that prayer, welcome to the family of God. Now find a good Bible-teaching church, attend faithfully, and let's look forward to what he is about to do in your life. For each of us who have accepted Jesus, whether that was five minutes ago or five years ago, the question now is will you or will you not serve him?

To serve or not to serve? That is the question!

THE ANSWER IS
Yes!

Randy and Terri's sons, Eric and Allen, in the midst of the destruction.

This picture says it all. Part of the destruction we saw in Oklahoma.

Randy and Terri Johnson   Tommy and Lisa Willis   Clyde and Carolyn Mangrum

Loading donated supplies for our first response.

Photos from Chapter 3

"YES" CAN FIX THIS

Randy with Brother Bess in his newly rebuilt home.

The newspaper clipping in the photo reads:

Hopes —

Continued from 1A

For Bess, the last two months have been full of fear and apprehension as surveyors have worked to determine whether Bess's home stands on a flood plain that could cause him to have to leave the land he has lived on for more than 48 years.

"I lost my wife on Dec. 15, 1998, after 51 years, and I didn't want to lose my home, too," Bess said. "I've been in a dread for the last month or so, just wondering what I was going to do because they told me I might not be able to build back."

McDaniel said because of the floods from Floyd, "the flood plains are changing."

Every single piece of flooded property must be surveyed to determine whether it falls in an area where reconstruction is a possibility or if destroying the home and moving in is the best possible option. Rebuilt in high-risk flood areas is sometimes not feasible because homeowners are required to elevate the structures one inch above what the surveyors determine the flood level to be.

For many people, including Bess, this is not possible because their homes are built on concrete slabs.

On this day, however, Bess's spirits are soaring. Earlier that morning, he found out his home — though only two houses away from property that people are being told they should leave the area — falls within an area where rebuilding is possible.

"I just got notice today that I could build back," Bess said, a smile lighting up his face as

"We've lost almost everything we've got, but the Lord has been good with the people He sent by to help."

the place, and my home was so unstable. It was just such a helpless feeling. All I could do was pray and hope for the best."

As Bess talked, a neighbor from down the road, 66-year-old Marta Hedgepath, popped into the house, leaning through what was once the living room wall, she began talking to Bess who sat in a green wooden kitchen chair across from the tiny black-and-white TV set in what used to be his kitchen.

Hedgepath asked if Bess got to keep his home, and told him, "I'm so glad you're going to be able to build your house back," after he said yes.

Hedgepath wasn't so lucky.

"I don't know what I'm going to do," she said. "I lost my home. I just found out this morning.

"We got an estimate, and it's going to be $10,000 to $20,000 just to elevate our home. They didn't advise me to build back, just to tear out."

However, such as Bess and hundreds of others in the Greenville area, Hedgepath has found comfort in prayer.

"We've lost almost everything we've got, but the Lord has been good with the people He sent by to help," Hedgepath said. "He sure taught me one thing I didn't like then. I thought I was set for my Golden Years, but now I really have to depend on Him."

Even though Bess can rebuild, there is still a ton of supplies Johnson needs and a lot funds he needs to raise to buy the supplies.

"I have a lot of friends who do carpentry and construction work. They've all volunteered their labor, but we still need to buy all the supplies," Johnson said. "If every person in Danville just skimped, cut out to

Brother Bess

Randy, Pastor Kevin and his father, and Clyde Mangrums putting the final touches to Brother Bess's bedroom.

Photos from Chapter 4

A DRIPPING POPSICLE

Five-year-old Jarrett

10-Year-Old Jarrett working on a home rebuild for a disabled lady.

Brantley Riddle, Jarrett Johnson, and other volunteers welcoming a Veteran to his new home built by God's Pit Crew.

Jarrett learning at an early age how to operate equipment.

Photos from Chapter 5

KMART AND KATRINA

God's Pit Crew set up trailers in front of the Danville K-Mart to collect supplies for Hurricane Katrina

Randy and Doug Young receiving an award for God's Pit Crew.

The God's Pit Crew warehouse with supplies that were collected for Hurricane Katrina.

Part of the Danville CERT Team that Doug pulled together to help manage God's Pit Crew's Katrina response.

Photos from Chapter 6

THE PRESENCE OF GOD

Supplies were delivered and organized for distribution.

Supplies being distributed to victims of Hurricane Katrina.

Randy is overcome with emotion after seeing the devastation from Katrina first-hand.

Some of the first sights of devastation the Crew saw after arriving in Gulfport, Mississippi.

Photos from Chapter 7

ALL WE COULD DO WAS PRAY

The Kinsey Family in their gutted home.

The Kinsey house during the rebuilding process.

The Kinsey family touring their finished home.

The Kinsey house after God's Pit Crew rebuilt it.

Photos from Chapter 8

STICKS, STONES, AND KNUCKLEBONES

God's Pit Crew built 8 homes for families in Haiti.

Recipients stand outside their new home.

Children play on a new playground built by GPC.

Haitian children receiving Gifts of Love.

Gifts of Love being assembled at the GPC distribution center.

Photos from Chapter 9

BE THE BLESSING

Volunteers assemble Blessing Buckets at GPC Distribution Center

Volunteers collecting supplies for Blessing Buckets at the annual
Blessing Bucket Drive.

Julie Burnett,
Blessing Bucket
Program Director
for God's Pit Crew

Blessing Bucket recipients following Hurricane Dorian in the Bahamas.

Photos from Chapter 10

ONLY A BOY

Jarrett on his first trip to Haiti at the IMO compound.

Jarrett visiting with students at IMO Schools.

Jarrett in 2014 at the site of the new school.

New school nearly complete.

THE REST OF THE STORY

Silas Zeidler

Trevor Dowdy   *Ethan Newlen*

David and Joanna Willis

James Hodge

God's Pit Crew 2019

God's Pit Crew's Home Base in Danville, Virginia

God's Pit Crew volunteers working together on rebuild projects.

Endorsements

Through the years, the Church of God has been blessed by God's Pit Crew in multiple emergencies across the land and even around the world. Without fail, God's Pit Crew has been the difference in bringing hope to the hopeless and help to the helpless. From most humble beginnings in 1999 to the significant impact now being made, God's Pit Crew continues to be a beacon of brilliant light, piercing the darkness of despair. I am proud to say that God's Pit Crew is recognized by the Church of God as one of our most significant partners in relief ministry. I look forward to continued partnership in the years to come.

—Timothy M. Hill, DD
General Overseer of the Church of God
Cleveland, Tennessee

*****

I am pleased to have this opportunity to recommend Randy Johnson and God's Pit Crew. Randy is a person of great compassion, character, and conviction. He models this both in his personal life and through the ministry of God's Pit Crew. Thomas Road has partnered with Randy and God's

Pit Crew for many years, both locally and nationally to assist and bring relief to those who have been affected by disasters. We have served together in San Leon, Texas, to rebuild a church that had been devastated by Hurricane Ike. In West Virginia, we partnered to assist flood victims and here in Lynchburg during the derecho. Recently, we partnered in rebuilding a home in Appomattox, Virginia, that had been destroyed by a tornado.

God's Pit Crew is marked by excellence in everything they do from personal professionalism to first-class equipment, to financial integrity. It is without any reservation that I am pleased to recommend Randy Johnson and God's Pit Crew to anyone who may be considering them for partnership and support. I consider Randy a great friend and look forward to our continued partnership in ministry for years to come.

—Jonathan Falwell
Pastor of Thomas Road Baptist Church
Lynchburg, Virginia

*****

I am pleased to write this letter of recommendation for Randy Johnson, the founder and director of God's Pit Crew. I had the privilege of meeting Randy during the recovery efforts of Superstorm Sandy in New York City. His efforts and those of his crew were invaluable to our city. Their efficiency in organizing and executing disaster relief is well recognized throughout the world. Randy is very organized and is responsible for coordinating teams under extreme circumstances with very little notice. With God's help and under Randy's leadership, God's Pit Crew has become one of the most competent and effective disaster relief teams in the world. He works tirelessly while maintaining focus and a positive attitude because he knows God is in the midst of it all. In addition to my ministry relationship with Randy, I have come to know him well on a personal level and consider him to be a real friend. I am pleased to recommend him and God's Pit Crew without any reservation.

—Alex Burgos
Associate Pastor of The Brooklyn Tabernacle
Brooklyn, New York

*****

It has been an honor for Mercy Chefs to partner with God's Pit Crew over the years. Their team is the definition of "hardworking" and has accomplished more for disaster victims in terms of long-term physical recovery than most any other organization in our field. We are proud to feed their teams so they can help communities across the country return to a new normal following disaster.

—Gary LeBlanc
Founder and President, Mercy Chefs
Portsmouth, Virginia

Hope.
Healing.
Restoration.

Our Mission:

WITH GOD'S HELP AND DIRECTION, TO BRING

HOPE, HEALING, AND RESTORATION

TO HURTING PEOPLE IN TIMES OF CRISIS.

What We Do

DISASTER RELIEF God's Pit Crew is ready, trained, and prepared to respond at a moment's notice after a disaster strikes.

BUILDING PROJECTS God's Pit Crew has taken on many building projects following a disaster, to help those who have lost everything.

BLESSING BUCKETS Blessing Buckets provide essential life- sustaining goods to people who have been displaced, or who are in need after a disaster.

LOCAL DISTRIBUTION Since 1999, we have distributed over 200 million pounds of food and supplies to 180 local nonprofit agencies that serve thousands in our community.

PHONE: (434) 836-4472   WWW.GODSPITCREW.ORG   EMAIL: CONTACT@GODSPITCREW.ORG

Does God's Pit Crew need your help?

THE ANSWER IS

Go to **www.godspitcrew.org**
to find out how!

CPSIA information can be obtained
at www.ICGtesting.com
Printed in the USA
JSHW012116120423
40183JS00004B/18